Our Trip to Mesa Verde 1922

Our Trip to Mesa Verde - 1922

by Ruth Miller

Ridgway, Colorado

U.S.A.

Publisher: Wayfinder Press, Ridgway, Colorado 81432

Printer: Country Graphics, Ridgway, Colorado U.S.A.
Book design: Pat Wilson, Country Graphics

Prologue

This small booklet was put together from three papers presented for a Literary Club assignment at Western State College in Gunnison, Colorado. We were members of the Delphians; our rivals were the Athenians. The year was 1922.

The paper, "Our Hiking Trip to Mesa Verde," was requested for one of the monthly programs required by the club. Since three of our four hikers were at Western State, we decided to divide our trip into three sections: The first was written by Edith Fetz ("Fetzie") of Hotchkiss, Colorado, whose parents were orchardists; the second by Ruth Hunsicker ("Ruth H.") of Eckert, Colorado, whose father was the principal of schools and the minister and builder of the Eckert Presbyterian Church; and the third part by me, Ruth Erickson ("Ruth E.") of the Highland Ranch of Ouray, Colorado, homesteaded by my grandparents, Marie and Alfred Forsman.

The three of us had been together at Western State and were all teaching in schools in the Delta area just before our southern Colorado trek. Ruth H. who taught school in Delta, introduced me to her father at summer school and he had hired me to teach in his school in Eckert. Dorothy Hunsicker

("Dot"), Ruth H.'s sister, added herself to our trio to make four. Harriet Pyle, the daughter of the Dolores Postmaster, who hosted us at his home, joined us to go to Mesa Verde. So now we were five.

Ruth H., Fetzie, and I naturally came together for the trip. We were always the ones who climbed the highest, ran the fastest, started all the games, and went on any hike that came to our attention. On one of these hikes, to the Waunita Hot Springs east of Gunnison, we invited Coach Krause and Stella Yowell, the primary professor, to go with us. They were thought of as extra good sports. We left Gunnison on a nice summer morning for the hotel and its swimming pool.

Coach Krause was most helpful. Ten of us started but one was sent back when Coach Krause noticed she was dressed in high heels, silk hose, and a light dress. He explained that she should leave the hike now, as it wouldn't be long before she would not be able to go back home. He told us that on long hikes, at rest stops, we should lie on our backs with our feet resting on a high place, such as a fence post or rock.

We made our own way on this hike, not following roads, but cutting across the sagebrush hills, so we didn't put in all that many miles on the car road. It was a wonderful weekend and a helpful experience for what was to come.

We taught school in Delta County that winter and spent some weekends together, always taking a long hike. It was then that Ruth H. and I decided to spend the month of June going to Mesa Verde to the Cliff Dwellings, which were just then being readied for visitors. We had been reading about the Indian ruins being excavated and studied at Mesa Verde. We decided it was the place to see.

We also decided it would be even better if we could have our pal from the summer before at Western State with us. We remembered how the three of us planned outings, picnics, climbs, and our memorable hike to Waunita Springs. So we drove to the Fetz home to tell her all about our plan. She and her two sisters entertained us with circus tricks on their pony.

We assured the Fetz family that our idea had been heartily endorsed by my parents, who were wishing they were free to go along. By this time Ruth H.'s younger sister, Dot, had decided to go along. Ruth H. and I were the most experienced outdoor people so we took over the planning for "Our Trip to Mesa Verde."

The "adventure" was written by three members of the trip — Part I by Edith Fetz ("Fetzie"); Part II by Ruth Hunsicker ("Ruth H."); and Part III, by Ruth Erickson ("Ruth E.").

—by Ruth E. (Ruth Erickson-Miller)

Part I
Seeking Adventure

I suppose people wonder how we ever came to take our walking trip to Mesa Verde. I believe, in the first place, Ruth H. dreamed about it and then she and Ruth E. became more enthused over the plan every time they talked about it. Of course, they included me in their plans, although I knew nothing about it until late in the spring, 1922.

On the second day of June, Ruth H., her sister Dot and I went to Ouray on the Denver and Rio Grande Railroad. Ruth E. met us at Lotus Switch and took us to her family's mountain ranch. We spent the time until the fourth, a Sunday, in making preparations. I remember what a good time we had rolling our packs and packing our kits Saturday night. If it hadn't been for Uncle Allie, Ruth E.'s soldier uncle, I'm afraid we would never have had as much success as we did. Ruth H. and I, of course, were the only ones to argue. I insisted on taking my p.j.s and the rest of them laughed at me. "We'll sleep out of doors most of the time and they'll be a nuisance," they said, but I took them just the same. Ruth H. insisted on taking iodine, foot dope, arch supports, adhesive tape,

Ruth E. with our .22,
Ruth H. with camera & supplies.

Dot & Fetzie;
the road stretches on and on.

"Easum", Sal Hepatica, soap, dress shoes and all sorts of what I called junk. I was sure if she put in all of those things there wouldn't be room for my manicure scissors, cutex, polish, etc. But there was!

Well, Sunday morning we were up early and we'd have been ready to start at 7:00 if I hadn't delayed to eat an extra egg which Mr. Erickson said I'd appreciate later in the day. We started from the ranch and all of that day, when we weren't going straight down, we continued to go straight up. Dot and I hadn't walked more than a block at one time all winter. We didn't have a real trail because the best trails were over the high country and were covered with snow. We only knew we were going in the general direction of Dallas Divide. When it seemed as if we had walked a million miles and it was almost dinner time, we came to a clearing and inquired of a man if we were going the right way. He assured us we were and that Beaver Creek, where we intended to eat our lunch, was only a few miles distance. At last we arrived. By this time Dot was limping, my heels were blistered and my hips were both rubbed raw from carrying a Boy Scout axe which Ruth H. said was perfectly necessary to cut wood and spruce boughs to make a bed or even some sort of a shelter. I might just mention that we used it once, at Lake

Ruth H. adjusting Ruth E.'s pack —
maybe pushing her along.

City, where we could have easily borrowed one.

Lunch surely tasted delicious, the chief thing desirable was quantity. It started to rain, but we had to stop long enough to pull off our boots and fill them with Easum. (Editor's Note: Easum is a powder said to be restful to tired feet.) By this time Dot and I had said, "Wait a minute, kids," so many times that our plea fell on deaf ears as far as the Ruths were concerned. About three o'clock I had begun to wish for home and mother, but mostly for my bedroom slippers. We passed one summer ranch house where the whole family was gathered and they looked at us as if we were curiosities. We got used to this quite soon. By this time we had begun to wonder where the farmhouse was where we intended to spend the night. When we asked a man, he told us that our destination was the second house on the left-hand side of the road. Of course, we were overjoyed, but our hopes were in vain for all the houses were on the right side of the road. Long before we reached our destination we had to resort to saying, "Walk a mile, rest a while, 21 miles from home," etc. (Editor's Note: In rhyme form, it continues: "walk a mile, rest a while, 22 miles from home;" then "23 miles from home," etc.) It didn't help much, but at least we saw the long-looked-for house.

I was glad to see Doris and Ula Brown, but

Mr. King & three of his grateful passengers.

The growing town of Redvale.

gladder to see and feel the couch. Supper was rather interesting, but couldn't hold a candle to the joys of the bathtub and all of Ruth H.'s foot dope. The blisters gained on that day stayed with me for many a long day. That was the nicest farm house, and we even had feather beds! The host and hostess of the night were friends of Ruth E.'s family from the days of the early settlers and homesteaders. Doris' parents, the Wards, and the Forsmans were early neighbors.

We were up and started fairly early and we weren't so very stiff, just rather. That was our lucky day, for about 9:30 that morning we got a lift with the county agent, Mr. King. We stopped at Placerville for lunch and then went on to Norwood. Mr. King found that his business took him on to Redvale, so we went, too. We arrived at this city of one store, the upstairs, a sort of hotel, about three o'clock. We had to have our exercise so we challenged the town team to a game of baseball, and of course, beat them. While we were resting and writing letters, two trucks came along loaded with men. They drove up to the store and our curiosity almost overcame our sense of ladylikeness. We resisted the temptation for a while and then went up to mail a letter. They were just leaving when the lady at the store told us we had missed our best chance for a ride as they were go-

Lumber wagon sans pillows.

*The Young Ranch —
all alone in the wide open spaces.*

ing fifteen miles in our direction.

We had talked to a Mr. Young at Placerville who owned a ranch in the middle of Dry Creek Basin. The next morning, after a rather good sleep in rather hard beds, we started out for this ranch. Our young boy-friends of the baseball game accompanied us and were getting a little out of hand, from the point of view of three school teachers, but Ruth E. gained their respect and admiration forever by shooting a rabbit with her trusty twenty-two. They soon faded away. We walked about five miles when a wagon loaded with lumber and drawn by four horses overtook us. The men were quite sympathetic and asked us to ride. We'd made up our minds never to refuse a ride, so we climbed on. After seven miles had been covered, our paths parted, and we started on foot.

We ate lunch under the bridge at Hamilton Creek because of rain. Ruth E.'s rabbit, well cooked but tough, was our chief item of food. Ruth H. favored the can of corn we opened. At last, when no ride appeared, we started and finally saw our long-looked-for landmark, a windmill. Mrs. Young received us very cordially and we engaged quarters in the hay barn for the night. After entertaining the family until after 9:30, we rushed out to the reservoir to take the moonlight bath we had promised ourselves ever since our arrival. Our one

The Young Ranch and another old Ford.

The camp area of the drilling operation.

blanket apiece wasn't sufficient that night and most of our time was spent asking, "Say, are you any warmer than I am?"

The next day was hot enough to make up for the night. We were nearing the Disappointment country, where nothing grows but silver sage and rattlesnakes interrupted by two or three water holes. We were just about to pass through Gypsum Gap when someone saw, in the distance, a cloud of dust. We settled down in the shade of a lone cedar to wait and see what was causing this. We decided that if it were a car, we'd hail it and ask where the next water hole was, in hopes of them asking us to ride. As it drew near, we saw that it was a car, so we put on our packs and started up the road. As it passed we shouted in unison, "Say...etc." They stopped and talked, and we got in. The occupants were two nice mining men and the car was a perfectly good Hupmobile. We rode about thirty-five miles with them and Mr. Burwell said we were certainly lucky for it was so hot in the valley during the day that he knew we could only have travelled by night. Near a point of rock, the young man who was driving, stopped the car and said, "There are so many rattlesnakes in this country I'm sure there is one at the top of that big cliff." He rushed up, went "Bang" with his revolver and said, "Come and see." It was a

Our quarters at the Beaumont Drill Camp.

The cook tent. We gals and the cook, Blair Burwell
(at right), and the boss, was later the president of
the Colorado Mining Association.

huge rattler alright, but he must have shot it on the way out the day before, because it was swollen from the heat. Ha!

Our luck continued to hold, for we spent the night at their mining camp half-way up Seven Mile Hill at Dolores Canyon. It was much like you read about in books, for each man brought his best blanket, his pillow, mattress or some such offering and they waited on us as if we were princesses. We spent a pleasant evening around a huge campfire on the edge of the canyon being entertained by their stories about tarantulas and such, and doing our part by a song or two.

We were awakened in the morning by the call, "Breakfast!" We washed the dishes for Mrs. Parr that morning. Every dish in camp was dirty, at least I thought we would never come to the end. In the course of the dishwashing I discovered my watch was missing and after every man in camp made an individual search, I discovered it in my pocket. At last we had to say good-bye and they insisted that if we'd come back that way they'd meet us at Dolores Canyon and take us back to Redvale. Saddest of all, we had to leave without saying good-bye to Clair, the younger of the two men, because he had not returned from a short, but necessary, survey.

In the course of the journey we came to a small

This is the diamond drill machine,
which brought up core samples.

After the dishes were done & packed for the move
to the next drilling site; Fetzie, Ruth E. & Ruth H.

schoolhouse in Egnar. We found a girl teaching there with thirty-eight children in all eight grades with no conveniences whatsoever. We visited with her and her class before heading on to Dove Creek. It was our ultimate destination that day but it seemed as if we'd never get there. Twenty-five long miles and then it began to get dark. When darkness had finally arrived the lights of Dove Creek came into sight. The first place we hit we discovered was a hotel and if they had known we were coming we'd have had the entire population, all male, out to meet us. We inquired for rooms and the proprietor led us up some squeaky stairs to a double room. We left our packs there and went down the street for some ice cream. It was mostly frozen milk but we were thankful even for that. On our return we asked for a place to wash and found that the bath was the size of the kitchen wash basin. We attempted to wash our faces and feet. I might mention that by this time the girls all envied me my p.j.s. After we crawled into bed and blew out the light we listened to the discussion going on around us. The cracks in the walls were rather huge and sound carried well. It seemed that Dove Creek hadn't seen so much excitement for a long time. We learned the next morning at the shoe shop that everyone knew about our movements, even to the ice cream shop. Dove Creek wasn't so bad! I got

Mr. Pyle, our host, sees his daughter off
with the four tramps to Mesa Verde.

The drugstore at Lewis.

my boots mended for nothing!

Next day was unlucky again as to rides. But walking wasn't crowded and we all felt dirty enough to be real tramps. The wind blew and dust wasn't scarce and all we saw were signs, "Deeded Lands For Sale — Cheap." Soon after that, however, it became valuable farm land, raising beans and then alfalfa. At last, just when we had stopped at a little creek to bathe our weary feet, a truck drove up and stopped for water. Dot still had on her shoes so she ran over and told a hard-luck story of blisters, stomach aches, etc., and we got a ride. After several more miles of desert we came to some green alfalfa fields and then the community of Lewis. There, we were offered unusual lodging. On a spur of a railroad stood a train sleeping-car with a cheerful little lady, the hostess. We slept in the sleeper bunks and had supper and breakfast in the dining part of the car. I don't think we even asked how the car got there, we were so pleased to be so well cared for. I think we each ate a dozen flapjacks for breakfast, but we were working people by then. We made friends with the fat druggist and he arranged for a ride for us to Dolores. Consequently, we arrived there in good season and Harriet, a friend of Ruth E.'s from high school in Fort Collins, was quite glad to see us. We stayed there for a few days enjoying the "Elk's

Harriet Pyle's cousin with his "harem."

We walk awhile, we rest awhile...

Annual," wearing borrowed clothes. Then, accompanied by Harriet, we set out for Mancos.

Oh yes, of course, we were all stricken with a slight attack of stomach trouble, having quenched our thirst from an irrigation flume, and by the time we arrived in Mancos I could go no farther. We saw a doctor who advised us to stay over a day. Ruth E. and Ruth H. were quite ambitious so they applied for a job in a restaurant, but found that it was a cook that was needed and, as they could not qualify, had to give up that idea. Glenn, Harriet's cousin, took us, his harem as his friends called us, to the picture show. The movie was "The Shiek of Araby." When the song written for the movie came on a local " violinist" played it. He could play using one finger, sliding it up and down the string. The movie house was a barn-like loft over a town store. The seating was folding chairs.

The next morning we made arrangements for a ride to the park. The road to Mesa Verde was a graded, narrow, one-way road. When someone started up a telephone call made sure no one was on the way down, after which, no one could start down until the caller arrived at the top. Our way from Mancos was on a supply truck, whose driver we smilingly cajoled into letting us ride on the produce boxes. We took a picture of the telephone booth at the bottom of Mesa Verde hill.

The supply truck into Mesa Verde
on which we rode. The price — five smiling faces.

The telephone booth at the foot of the one-way road
into Mesa Verde. A call that a vehicle is on the
way up, keeps cars from coming down.

Part II
In the Park

It was nearly noon when we reached the park and stopped to look at the latest ruins which Dr. Fewkes was then excavating. He named it "New Fire House." There seemed to be a number of other mounds which Dr. Fewkes said they would eventually excavate. These new ruins, the "Far View House" and the "Sun Temple," differ from the others by being on top of the mesa and not in the canyons.

Dr. Fewkes is the archeologist from the Smithsonian Institute. He has done a great deal toward unearthing these ruins, explaining the reasons for the things found and also in explaining the disappearance of these "Little People," as the Indians call the Cliff Dwellers.

Just before we arrived they had unearthed eight pieces of pottery, corn, feather cloth, implements, skulls, other bones, etc. Dr. Fewkes told us all about the things and then climbed to the top of the wall to have his picture taken.

From there we went on to the hotel. It was a low frame building in which the dining room and office were located. The Museum was a

The porch overlooking Spruce Tree House, the first
& only permanent building in 1922.

Dr. Fewkes & our group
at the site of his present work.

beautiful log building overlooking the canyon where "Spruce Tree House" is located. The sleeping apartments were tents. We five girls took one tent and proceeded to make ourselves at home; our home, on the whole trip, being just where our packs were off, hillside or hotel. After lunch the guide, Roger Owen, who was acting chief ranger, suggested a tour of some of the lesser ruins. We went in a Ford truck over the flat mesa and thru the cedars. Riding along those drives one would never suspect that a canyon was near, especially the deep ones which cut the whole mesa. We headed for these canyons where one could see down for hundreds of feet. We left the truck and climbed down into the canyon, then up ladders and perpendicular rock walls to the ruins. Those we visited that afternoon were "Willow Tree House" and "Oak Tree House."

In our party that afternoon were some tourists visiting these scenes for the first time. All afternoon we heard, "Oh! Elmer! We ain't never seen anything like this before!" "Oh! Elmer! Can't you hear? The young man's talking," and so it continued.

One of the funniest things that happened was when Fetzie, as usual, tried to cut me out with the guide, Roger. You see, he was a most interesting young man, and I, in my thirst for

A guided tour with Roger, the Park Ranger,
Harriet, Fetzie, Ruth H. & Ruth E.

Our group, with Roger, at the Spruce Tree Camp
House, diningroom & sales office—
a temporary structure.

knowledge, stuck close to his side to hear his explanation of the various ruins. Fetzie, in her determination to cut me out, even sacrificed being near him herself, tried to push Dot or Ruth E. between us, but all to no avail. I stayed that time, in spite of the giggling from the other girls.

The ruins we visited that afternoon were mostly small ones. We found various rooms, a kiva or two, and the well-worn stones where they ground their corn and also the ones where they sharpened their axes.

In the evening, after Dr. Fewkes' lecture, the young men of the camp, the two guides and an archaeologist, proposed a trip to the "Tree House" by moonlight. We crossed the canyon and followed the edge of the mesa a short distance and came to a cliff. This we descended on a rope ten or fifteen feet. From the end of the rope we climbed down the branches of a huge spruce about fifteen feet. Then we came to the ledge on which this ruin was built. It was a very small one, on this very narrow ledge, and was of interest chiefly because of it's inaccessability. We spent a most pleasant hour there, singing and listening to the stories of "Nick," a most admirable story-teller. One of his stories concerned the spirits of the departed inhabitants of this house. It was simply blood-curdling. Another thing of interest here was the

The day we spent with children —
pretending we were cliff dwellers.

echo. "Nick" demonstrated this by shouting "Board of Health!" We were much surprised by the startling reply of the echo.

The next day we spent exploring. In the morning we went to "Cliff Palace, " one of the most wonderful of the ruins. It was three hundred feet long and had two hundred rooms, round and square towers, and kivas. It also had a subterranean entrance. We spent the entire morning playing around there with several small boys. They were children who accompanied us from the hotel, playing hide-and-seek and pretending to be cliff-dwellers. The round tower here was the only one yet discovered. The kivas were of great interest. They were round with six rock abutments representing the six directions; up, down, north, east, south, and west. At one side was a place for the ceremonial fire. Just behind it was the ventilation opening with a fire screen between it and the fire. Another thing of interest was a hole in the floor through which they talked with the evil spirits in order to pacify them when they were angry. All these kivas were originally covered with a roof of poles and bark with rocks over it. The means of entrance into the kivas was by ladder from the top or from a hole in the floor.

The doors and windows of these ruins were remarkable for their size and shape. They were very

One of the Mesa Verde ruins.

Our group & the archaeologists
who worked with Dr. Fewkes, all college men.

small and usually square or rectangular. The doors were sometimes "T" shaped so that a person with a pack could enter. To enter some, one had to swing from a well-worn pole. Most of the doors were high from the floor and were entered by a ladder which was made by cutting notches on logs. Things were very well preserved, probably due to the dry climate. We found corn, bones, feather cloth, grass mats and other things in good condition in the ruins, even after six hundred years.

In the afternoon, we went to the "Spruce Tree House" and spent a nice time exploring and reading in some cozy corners we found there. In the late afternoon we went to "Square Tower House." To get there, we had to go through the "Needles Eye." I imagine a very large person would have trouble getting through. We even expected Ruth E. to have difficulty, but she didn't. At "Square Tower" we found a ruin high up on the cliff called "Eagle's Nest." Several of us made up our minds to climb up in spite of the guides' declaration that it was dangerous and against the rules. We climbed it and got safely down again feeling quite repaid for our efforts by the wonderful view of the canyon and the green clad hills.

We visited the "Sun Temple," which was one of the most recent and most wonderful of the ruins. It had never been finished. It had been construct-

Harriet Pyle & Roger:
they corresponded all the rest of their lives.

ed as a fortress and a temple. It had only one means of access and that was well protected. At one side we saw a fossil palm leaf embedded in a stone, which these ancient people thought to be a divinely carved image of the sun. The masonry of this building showed a marked advance in civilization.

That same evening the crowd from the hotel had a marshmallow toast on the brink of Spruce Canyon. "Nick,' the storyteller, again related many interesting stories of spirits of these departed people. One story was just reaching it's most thrilling climax when a wrathy voice from the only camp asked, "Say, when do we sleep?" That relieved the tension but spoiled the story. Soon after that, Mr. Neusbaum, the Supervisor for the Park, took us down to see the wonderful home which he and Mrs. Neusmaum had built. It was an imitation of a cliff dwelling. The furniture had all been made by him, mostly of aspen wood, leaving, as much as possible, the weathered, silvery look. The fireplace was a replica of some found in the cliff dwellings. Mrs. Neusbaum was very interesting and could tell many stories about her Indian brothers as she was reared in an Indian tribe. Their small son sang Indian songs for us.

Mr. Smith, a Fetz family friend, took us for our good day in Ignacio and the Indian Bear Dance.

Ute Indian at the Bear Dance grounds.

Part III
The Homeward Journey

After leaving the park we went directly to Durango where we engaged a large room at a modern hotel, the Sheraton. We were used to hotels such as Dove Creek offered, so we wondered what the button on the wall was for. Just to find out, Ruth H. pushed it. Soon, there was a discreet knock at the door. The state of my dress was such as not to permit visitors so I ducked behind the bed. Ruth H. went to the door and, behold, the porter. Ruth H.'s presence of mind did not desert her and she gave our boots to be polished. When he had gone, we found that I had had the wrong estimation of the height of the bed and had hidden in true ostrich fashion. Our lack of robes was rather noticeable in our rambles to the bath room. Our blankets made valuable substitutes.

We later met friends there and were invited to stay. We went with them to Ignacio to see the Annual Bear Dance. This is a festival celebrated every spring by the Ute Indians as a sort of mating ceremony. It no longer has the same meaning that it once had, however. Ignacio is a village about thirty miles south of Durango. It was more like I had

The Utes constructing the circular enclosure of aspens which shielded the dances from view.

A chained bear cub.

imagined the old frontier villages to be than any I had ever expected to see. We arrived too early for anything to be happening, so we drove on south toward the border of New Mexico. We passed several dry ranches on which we saw queer old adobe houses. When we came back, the Indians had begun to gather from all around the country. There was a large meadow which was reserved for the Indians in which they were to meet. A large, circular brush enclosure had been constructed in which they were to have their dance. All the Indians sat placidly under the trees. A very few talked with their neighbors, but most of them looked as though the fate of the universe was bound up in their thoughts.

One old Indian sat on his horse, in the sun, with his heavy Navajo blanket tucked tightly around him, smoking a pipe. In contrast to this a young girl sat in a wagon in the shade of a tree, with a green parasol over her as added protection from the sun, playing with a rubber band on which a ball was tied. We drove down the road, past the government offices and the Indian school, and on past the place where the Utes have their annual Sun Dance, then came back past the Indian gathering. Everyone was exactly where he or she had been before. The girl still played with the ball and the Indian's pipe had not yet been finished.

The Ute Indian baseball pitcher
agreed to pose with us.

The dancers lined up for the Bear Dance.

There was to be a baseball game in the afternoon with Ignacio's team and the Indian team on the other side. We went, of course. The Indians won and George, the good natured pitcher allowed us to have our picture taken with him.

After the game we went down to the Bear Dance. It was already in progress. As we came near we heard a weird droning sound that reminded us of a farmer and his family hiving a swarm of bees. On entering we found that it was the orchestra. The music was produced by four old Indian men sitting around a large tin affair that resembled a wash tub. On this they braced notched sticks about two feet long which they rubbed with a bone in time to the music. The melody was carried by the really fine, deep bass voices of the men. One melody of eight measures of four-four time was repeated over and over again until the dancers were exhausted.

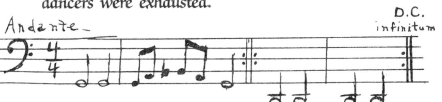

As we came in, a dance was just beginning. In this dance squaws chose their partners. Some were very bashful. The generally accepted way was for the young (or sometimes old) squaw to look in the direction of her choice and flip her finger or

Indian Man

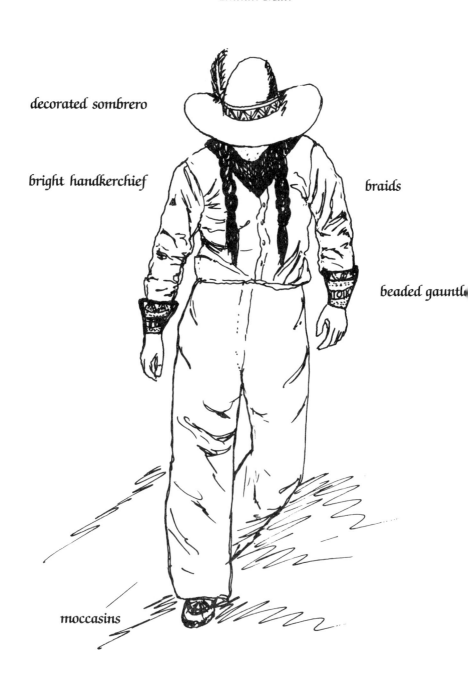

decorated sombrero

bright handkerchief

braids

beaded gauntl

moccasins

the corner of her blanket at him. He then accepted by stepping into the line opposite her.

Two lines were formed facing one another. The braves in one line and the squaws in the other. The music started and they began. The lines advanced and retreated until someone was so tired he or she had to stop, their place taken by another.

One old squaw with a blanket, moccasins, beads, earrings, and an old-fashioned Leghorn sailor hat perched rakishly on her head, invited a Durango banker to dance with her and, fearing to hurt her feelings, he did. When the dance ended, she asked him very politely for a quarter.

The costumes were the most interesting I have seen. Here and there an attempt to be like the whites was seen. One old dandy wore a striped silk shirt, blue serge trousers, a Stetson hat with a beaded band, two long black braids tied with beads, beaded moccasins and a sash of buckskin. To complete the queer costume he wore huge earrings.

We saw one squaw with a purple silk parasol, a red silk dress made in bungalow apron style, moccasins and earrings. She had attempted to be more like white folks by adding a bit of color to her cheeks. Well, perhaps it was more than a bit, but it was there, anyway. An old brave demonstrated a new style in shirts. He wore his with the tail out of his buckskin trousers. He had a sort of band,

Trimble Springs, a hot springs north of Durango.

The valley east of Silverton as we started over Engineer Mountain.

on his head, of fur with a feather perched jauntily up in back. He wore moccasins, earrings and many beads. His face was painted in real war paint.

We made several attempts to get pictures, but the Indians did not appreciate a Kodak, so we didn't get good ones as they were taken from under cover.

We returned to Durango that evening and started for Silverton the next day. We went swimming in the open air pool at Trimble Springs. We hadn't gone far when a high school boy and his small cousin passed us in a car. They stopped and asked if we wanted a ride. We didn't refuse. He told us he was going as far as Silverton.

Our party was one of the first to cross the range that spring. The road had been cut out of deep banks of snow. In one place we were stuck for a short time. We stayed in Silverton that night. When we first got there, we went to the store at the Post Office to get some ice cream. The entire population decided that they just had to get their mail at that particular moment. We had friends there and when we asked about the conditions of the mountain trails the women said, "Oh, you'll never be able to get to Lake City." The men said, "Well, there has been one man over already this spring. I think you can make it."

We travelled all the next day, stopping at two places, the only ones inhabited. At one place

Just about over the huge snow slide area with
Evelyn Yooch, who escorted us.

Packing up at Rose's Cabin to go into Lake City.

there was a young girl who was very nice. She walked with us for about five miles. This was across a huge snow slide. The next place was Animas Forks, a mining town, which had a population of three. We crossed Engineer Mountain that day which has an altitude of over fourteen thousand feet. From the top, one could see snow-capped peaks in all directions; to the south, the Silverton mountains; to the northwest, those of Ouray; and toward the northeast, the Lake City mountains and Hansen Creek, the way leading to Lake City.

There were several moments where there seemed to be a crisis. One came just before nightfall as we were approaching Rose's Cabin from the top of Engineer Pass. The mountain stream was quite a torrent from the melting snow. It separated us from the night's shelter, which would have been a freezing experience if we had tried to ford it. I found a long, strong stick which served as a vaulting pole and, Lo! we were safely across.

There was a caretaker in charge who said he knew my father. We girls were given lodging in the big, rambling mine bunk house. We had a wide choice of rooms. For the winter, the beds had been pulled up almost to the ceiling. Four of them were let down for us. We made biscuits, after carefully washing the tables and utensils. Fetzie, who had

The Lake San Cristobal cabin.

Hanging up the wet clothing;
wearing the only dry ones at the cabin.

always insited on being an old maid, said that she'd condescend to marrying one of the stockholders of the mine, so that she could spend her summers there.

The next morning the man decided to go to Lake City to get more provisions instead of staying to clean camp. He, of course, was going to take his mule and his horses, so we got to ride the full sixteen miles, I remember distinctly. You see, there were four saddles for the five of us so I rode bareback. I was happy to ride the little mule because the horses were fitted with pack saddles. We found the people of Lake City absolutely lovely. One family had a taffy pull for us and a nice old man loaned us a cabin at Lake San Cristobal and took us boating. Then fish, oh, we ate so many. Of course, we're not telling how many we ourselves caught.

One day we all washed our hair and went out in a boat on the Lake to dry it. We were way out in the middle when a storm came up and before we could get to shore we were drenched. Being soaked was an awful predicament when extra clothing was miles away at home in the clothes closet. Well, we washed, since our clothing was already wet, and ironed part of them dry. Having to dry out made us lose out on a fish supper to which we had been invited.

Ruth E., Fetzie, & Ruth H. near the train station
with the La Veta Hotel in the background.

The last stop before going home was Gunnison. The experience we had between Lake City and Gunnison made us expert Ford-pushers. Summer school was in progress so we saw many friends from the previous summer, many wishing they could have been to Mesa Verde with us. We had made plans to go over to Crested Butte, take Somerset Road to Hotchkiss and from there go home, but circumstances at home caused us to change our minds. We went home on the train, leaving one another along the way.

One thing that was discovered from our trip was that there are nice, friendly people everywhere, if one only takes the trouble to find them.

Back home in Gunnison
with a Western State College schoolmate

Ruth Miller
with grandson Dr. Edward Conrad,
daughter Ruthabeth, and great grandsons.

Epilogue

An epilogue written in 1988 is sixty-six years too late. Distance separated our group for many years, so it is difficult to write much about those who were not near.

Harriet Pyle of Dolores, Colorado and the young Park Ranger, Roger, started a correspondence that continued for years, each going separate ways, marrying and still writing to one another. Dorothy Hunsicker married Gilbert Doughty soon after we arrived home. He wasn't taking chances on Dot leaving on any more month-long trips without him. They made their home in Grand Junction, he being a dealer in heavy mining and road machinery. There were several children and, now, many grandchildren. Dot was a great asset to the musical community, having a lovely voice. They now live on the high ground across Surface Creek from the church her father planned and worked in.

Edith Fetz continued to teach for a number of years, though she married Edgar Byle a few years after our Mesa Verde trip. He was a builder of homes. They had one son. She was a valued person in her community of Hotchkiss.

Ruth Hunsicker taught in the valley for several

years until, while on a summer vacation trip to California, she met a tall, handsome young man who was living at the inn where she stayed. Joe Hunt and his family were building contractors. There was a lovely wedding at the Eckert church with Dot as a flower girl and I as maid of honor. The Hunts lived in California through the depression and in thankfulness for their success have built and given a church to their community of Burbank. They parented four fine people.

I returned to Western State in the fall after our trip to Mesa Verde along with Ruth H. and Fetzie. We and a couple of other girls always had a good time going to the Post Office. Our way went past a house in which a young man lived who saw us occasionally. He decided he would like to know the blonde of the group, which was I. This he did at a college dance. A mutual friend introduced me to Theodore Krueger.

When Theodore asked me if I would like to go for a drive on Sunday to see the fall colors my reply was "Miss Spicer, our Dean of Women, doesn't allow dormitory girls out in cars with young men." This was true, as unlikely as it now sounds. The young man said, "Just ask her if you would be allowed to go out with Theodore Krueger. I'll call you tomorrow." This I said I would do.

Miss Spicer said, "With whom did you say?"

When I repeated it, to my surprise she said, "Well, of course, you may." I then had to discover who this paragon of integrity was. The man I thought was a travelling salesman was the youngest U.S. Forest Supervisor in the country. He had been sent to Gunnison to settle the sheep and cattle war that was then being bitterly waged. He had done so by showing them that cattle would graze on land that had grazed sheep and that the forest land could be assigned to the stock for whom it was best suited. He was the Commander of the local American Legion and a member of the Rotary Club, where his nickname was T.K.

I found T.K. to be a fine and considerate person. By February I was persuaded to meet him in Denver where he was at a conference. My classmates received a telegram on February 11, 1923 that read, "Ruth was married this morning," signed, Ruth. Ruth H. was my bridesmaid.

We enjoyed the outdoors, the college advantages, our daughter, Ruthabeth, and a trip to Europe. When Ruthabeth was six years old the Forest Service took us to the Black Hills of South Dakota for about ten years. One of my hobbies was teaching Ruthabeth to play the violin. We moved to Denver where my old violin teacher, Howard Reynolds, became my daughter's teacher. It was time well spent. By the time she was sixteen she was winning national prizes.

After we moved to Denver, T.K. and I had built a very lovely home northeast of Denver. We enjoyed it several years before T.K. was stricken with a fatal heart attack. I was drafted to fill in as a teacher during a teacher shortage in Denver. After that one year I was persuaded not to teach again, instead to marry a man I had known all my life.

Ernest Miller had been a protégé of my father, who had persuaded him to go to Denver University for a business career. Our families had been in touch over the years. In Denver we had banked where Ernest worked. We had twelve wonderful years together and my grandchildren had a much loved grandfather.

As a high school girl in Fort Collins, Colorado I had studied violin and continued in music at Western State. In Denver I became a member of the Denver Symphony and continued for 29 years. My home now is Ouray, where my roots are. I live in a one-hundred-year-old house which T.K. and I bought years ago and Ernest made quite habitable. I spend winters in Arizona where I play in the Mesa Symphony, the Fine Arts Strings, and other chamber music. I visit my family in the far corners of the United States quite often and they enjoy Ouray.